REVOLUTIONARY PORTRAITS ■ DIEGO RIVERA

2

The Night of the Rich, Ministry of Education (Court of the Fiestas), Mexico City, 1926.

The Night of the Poor, Ministry of Education (Court of the Fiestas), Mexico City, 1926.

Diego Rivera: the man who painted walls *Mike Gonzalez*

First published in *International Socialism* 38, Spring 1988

This edition published in 2001 by

REDWORDS

1 Bloomsbury Street, London WC1B 3QE

www.redwords.org.uk

ISBN: 1 872208 13 4

Design and production by Roger Huddle

Printed by Interprint Ltd, Malta

Diego Rivera:
the man who painted walls

Mike Gonzalez

The Struggle of the Classes,
National Palace, Mexico City, 1935.

Publisher's note

This book is one of the first in a major series of **Revolutionary Portraits** from Redwords. The unifying theme in this eclectic collection is Marxism. Each author reviews the artist and their art in historical context. The focus is on the relationship between individual artists and larger historical forces, how each influences and shapes the other. All of the books in this series aim to lead us back to these works of art and music with new eyes and ears, and a deeper understanding of how art can raise the human spirit.

Others books in the current series are: Mozart Rembrandt and John Coltrane.

Redwords is a publishing collective specialising in art, history and literature from a socialist perspective. We are linked to Bookmarks.

Overleaf: *The Distribution of Arms*, Ministry of Education (Court of the Fiestas), Mexico City, 1928

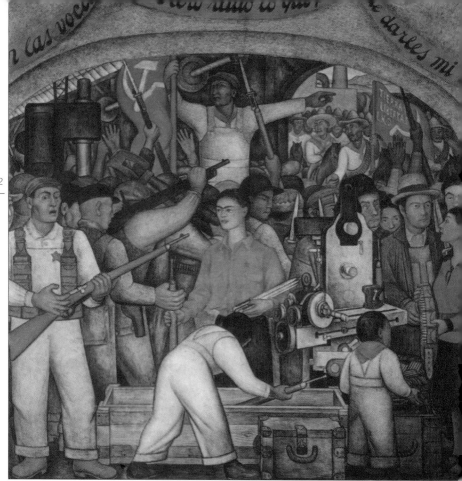

REVOLUTIONARY PORTRAITS

Art and revolution

Every revolution has its artists—those who sing its urgent and immediate songs, as well as those who tell its story as history. In Russia, after the October Revolution, Anatoly Lunacharsky sat in a freezing Comissariat for the Enlightenment,[1] and planned an extraordinary strategy for a revolutionary art. Some of the artists who sympathised with the revolution boarded the propaganda trains covered in posters and revolutionary graffiti, and carried their instant images of revolution to the remotest places. They produced the fine posters, the instant poems, the revolutionary songs and street plays that Mayakovsky celebrated. This was the army of the arts[2]—the agitational art of the revolutionary moment—inspiring and

1 Lunacharsky's own ideas are found in A Lunacharsky, *On Literature and Art* (Moscow, 1973). See also S Fitzpatrick, *The Comissariat of the Enlightenment* (Cambridge, 1980).

2 The phrase belongs to the great revolutionary poet Mayakovsky. In his poem *Order No 2 to the Army of the Arts,* he says, 'There are no fools today/to crowd, open mouthed, round a 'maestro'/and await his pronouncement./Comrades,/give us a new form of art——/an art/that will pull the republic out of the mud.' See D Widgery, 'Mayakovsky and Revolutionary Art', in *International Socialism* 1:52 (July/September 1972).

3 Quoted in A Strigalev, 'Art de propagande revolutionnaire, agitprop', in *Paris-Moscou 1900-1930* (Paris, 1979), pp314-336. See too Millon and Nochlin, (eds), *Art and Architecture in the Service of Praxis* (MIT, 1978). On the artistic environment of post-revolutionary Russia see the above, and C Gray, *The Russian Experiment in Art 1803-1922* (London, 1962). On the debates see Trotsky, *Literature and Revolution* (Redwords, 1985).

14

mobilising the Russian proletariat and peasantry to support the revolution.

But there was also another conception of what a revolutionary art should be—providing a vision of a socialist future, a promise of a deep and far-reaching transformation. It could only be represented in broad strokes, in sweeping prophecies, in monumental dreams. It seems strange now that Lissitsky and Tatlin produced sketches and blueprints for huge modern monuments—like Lissitsky's 300 foot high Speaker's Platform for Lenin—when Petrograd had no electricity and the White armies were burning crops in the Ukraine. Even stranger, perhaps, that Lenin should in 1918 have presented a resolution to the Central Committee of the Communist Party entitled 'On Monuments',[3] quoting from the visionary texts of Thomas Campanella, the medieval mystic.

Yet there was behind it all a deep and compelling logic. In times of hardship, the working class can be sustained by a promise delivered with conviction, a prophecy reinforced with certainty. The sketches envisioned the future—they were the reward that history offered. Later, of course, those monumental promises were turned on their head and made falsifications, lies, illusions. The statues of Stalin and his approved heroes had nothing to do with the continuity of revolutionary tradition that Lenin had talked about in his plan to distribute statues of great revolutionaries around the streets. When the monuments were divorced from the practices of social organisation— when the paintings and sculptures in the streets no longer bore any relation to the language and vision that inspired the mass organisations, they became objects again, external things to be seen, admired, revered, but not used in the struggle. The workers of Moscow could be impressed by the grandeur of the Moscow underground, but there was nothing in this imperial spectacle that pointed to a world that the workers would create for themselves.

Yet those first few years of the Russian revolution in art, long since abandoned by the inheritors of the patrons of Tatlin and others, established an idiom, an artistic language that has been imitated a hundred times since. Perhaps imitated is too mechanical a term. To put it another way, every period of significant social transformation has produced an art that reinforced, organised and responded to that process.

In each of these movements the painting of public places, the attempt to display a narrative of change on the walls of buildings, has been a recurring form. In Spain in 1936 posters often of daring and powerful design picked up the innovations of German designers

4 Many of the Spanish postcards have been reproduced by Leeds Postcards. They are reprinted in D Mitchell, *The Spanish Civil War* (London, 1982).

5 On Chile see C Barker et al, *Revolutionary Rehearsals* (London, 1987).

16

earlier in the decade.[4] In Chile after 1970 anonymous teams named after a murdered art student called Ramona Parra toured the streets and painted a continuous gallery of faces and forms, in great sweeping lines and hard bright colours, on the walls and fences around the shanty towns. The images reappeared on the banners that punctuated the huge demonstrations of the Popular Unity period.[5] In Portugal in 1975 huge murals appeared in cities and rural areas, like the painted reproduction of the famous portrait of Guevara that appeared on the side of an expropriated farmhouse in the Alentejo. In Mozambique the same huge portraits appear to commemorate the prehistory of revolution.

Yet the most persistent, the most widely known and perhaps the most influential of all the public art movements is the so called Mexican Mural Renaissance led and defined by three profoundly different and conflicting painters—Jose Clements Orozco, David Alfaro Siqueiros and Diego Rivera.

Walls inside and out

There can be little doubt that the Mexican Muralists represented one of the most significant movements in 20th century art. It was not that they transformed the techniques of painting, nor that their methods of work were particularly new. Their techniques and forms were, as they themselves insisted, among the very oldest. Rivera was adamant, for example, about the continuity between the Muralists of the 1920s and the anonymous artists of ancient Mexico who had decorated the inner chambers of the pyramids with frescoes of gods, kings and mythical creatures.[6] Orozco, on the other hand, pointed to another muralist tradition—the curious paintings that decorate the walls of Mexico's *pulquerias* (bars). When Rivera returned to Mexico from Europe in 1921 to begin his mural painting career, it was after a lengthy visit to Italy and the great murals of Florence and Rome. It was the techniques of the Italian Renaissance fresco masters that he used—painting directly onto wet plaster—and it was often their forms and figures that he imitated.[7]

So there was nothing new about painting walls. Except that the art of Europe had long since moved from walls to easels, and developed theories and explanations

6 The most complete examples are in the so called Butterfly Room in the Pyramid of the Moon at Teotihuacan.

7 The early part of Rivera's life is dealt with in several places, but in general the best overview of his work is B Wolfe, *Diego Rivera* (New York, 1939), and *Diego Rivera: A Retrospective* (New York/London,1987). For a different slant, and often a doubtful one, see B Moss, *The Big Wall* (London, 1979).

17

8 For more on this discussion see the first essay of John Berger's marvellous *Ways of Seeing* (London, 1972).

of the artistic process that corresponded to this essentially private and domestic form of art. Paintings were hung inside houses where they became part of the furniture, distinguished above all by their uniqueness and their monetary value. What mattered was to *own* them.[8] There was a paradox here. All the ideas about art that circulated then (and now) emphasised the uniqueness of the art object, the distance between artists and the rest of the human race. They were 'inspired', living apart, they had a 'creative instinct or urge' which drove them. They were exempt from work, and were not condemned as others were as feckless and anti-social because they opted to starve. Of course this was because of this curious indefinable individuality that enclosed them in the garrets and Bohemias of a bourgeois age. For artists that uniqueness was, in one guise or another, a reaction against the drive of capitalism to render everything, every human being, a saleable commodity—one component in a great productive apparatus. It was couched in terms of an individuality refusing to be placed in the machine. Yet that very refusal was turned into a sellable commodity, as the uniqueness of the painting guaranteed its increasing market value.

At the turn of the century that rebellion, that refusal to be sucked into a culture of goods, bought and sold, of mass production and factories, became increasingly radical. Art withdrew further and further into itself, refusing to represent the world of the bourgeois. Yet artists still lived on the patronage of the collecting classes—and their closed visions of the world were still bought and sold like so many stocks and shares. So the avant garde art of the beginning of the 20th century made its rebellion explicit as well as implicit in the frame. Dada laughed at the bourgeoisie—charged them entrance to their exhibitions and then laughed in their faces. It broke down art itself, made it unsellable, parodied the commodity—like Man Ray's photograph of the iron with nails in it. It was the most far-reaching expression of that comprehensive rebellion against the authority of the bourgeois world. Yet in the end it was a rebellion of individual artists taking personal positions of marginality and rejection. Their explanations of their rebellion were aristocratic and elitist, though some did try to establish an analogy between their own refusal to cooperate with the prevailing ideas and the working class. Yet for the most part they had little or no organic contact with that class, and only barely understood its needs and drives. Perhaps unknowingly, they were reflecting the great upsurge in working class struggle throughout Europe of 1911-14. But their rebellion remained an act

9 See note 3. Also L Claudin Urondo, *Lenin and the Cultural Revolution* (Brighton, 1977).

10 He argued in *Literature and Revolution*, 'It is childish to think that bourgeois "belles lettres" can make a breach in class solidarity. What the worker will take from Goethe, Pushkin or Shakespeare will be a more complex idea of human personality.' L Trotsky, op cit, p225.

11 Cf Lenin's articles on Tolstoy, M Soloman, *Marxism and Art*, (New York, 1972).

20

of personal solidarity, and their paintings, though sometimes visionary, little more than personal statements.

Until 1917 the revolution in art made little contact with the art of revolution. After October the great leap to bring together art and struggle began in earnest. In Russia and outside there were debates about the content of this new art and debates about its form.[9] Proletcult argued that the new culture should use only the material of proletarian experience, rejecting everything that was the product of the bourgeois past. Other schools sympathised to a greater or lesser degree with this view of a new art—collective in aspiration, proletarian in content and embedded in its practices the construction of the new socialist order. Art would mobilise, agitate, recreate the physical and ideological environment, inform and encourage. And it would also be prophetic, delivering an outline of the future world.

Lenin and Trotsky[10] were deeply suspicious of such blind utopianism. The past was not alien, they argued. Human history was also the history of the emergence and growth of the working class, the source and explanation of its actual consciousness, and the fruit of its experience. To ignore what *is* in favour of what *will be* is a formula for impotence. In Russia, Lenin argued, in discussing Tolstoy,[11] the proletariat must first learn its own history and take possession of all that humanity has been able to produce in its struggle for progress. Russia could create a new culture when, and only when, it had appropriated the old.

In Russia the debate on the nature of a revolutionary art was interwoven with the political issues arising out of the October Revolution. Art was a weapon in the construction of socialism. The immense authority of the Bolshevik Revolution extended to prescriptions for a new art. Its echoes reached into revolutionary movements throughout the world, but the sound was a little late in reaching Mexico, where a revolutionary upheaval that began in 1910 had reached, in 1917, a resolution unfavourable to the working class as a whole. Yet the precepts of revolutionary art were taken up and expounded in Mexico and that art, for very particular reasons, not only drew on the experience of 1917 but in a sense systematically rewrote its history.

The Mexican revolution

The year 1910 was the centenary of Mexico's formal separation from Spain and its establishment as an independent state. In the intervening 100 years Mexico had reintegrated into the world economy through the relations between the Mexican bourgeoisie and British and French capital. Its natural resources had been the subject of a series of armed conflicts between representatives of distinct foreign interests, yet the resolution of each battle served not to set Mexico on the road to development or modernisation, but ensured its continuing absorption into the structure of foreign capital investment. By 1910 Mexico exhibited the combination of modern and backward sectors characteristic of colonial economies. Imperialism in its European form had provided the technology and the capital with which to develop mining and oil exploration on the one hand, and (in partnership with the Mexican landowning class) to develop the export sector in agriculture on the other. A Mexican middle class had emerged in its turn, acting as agents of foreign capital or supplying local inputs for foreign industry. Culturally, that middle class aspired to full integration into the European bourgeoisie. Their sons and daughters went to Paris to be educated, while they themselves remained in Mexico and created a kind of imitation Paris—bringing over the most fashionable opera and theatre companies, and reproducing in their houses and streets the arcades and galleries of Paris.

On the land Mexico wore a very different face. American journalist John Kenneth Turner[12] described how the workers on the tobacco and coffee plantations of the Atlantic coast were tied in virtual slavery through the system of debt peonage. In the south captive labour struggled to harvest the henequen plant in Yucatan, but very few survived the intense heat. And in the centre of the country, in the state of Morelos, the profitable sugar plantations expanded their borders, and absorbed and destroyed the peasant communities that stood in their way.[13] These interests found an ally and protector in Porfirio Diaz, whose 30-year dictatorship had overseen a process of modernisation financed and governed by foreign interests.[14] New laws were obligingly passed, like that of 26 March 1894 which permitted foreign companies to occupy what were loosely defined as 'unused lands'—and they found more than 50 million acres of such land during the Diaz regime.

By 1910 Diaz had brought to completion a kind of economic development,[15] but it was uneven, beneficial

12 J K Turner, *Barbarous Mexico*, (New York, 1907). The book was widely read both in Mexico and the US. Turner himself was a radical journalist who posed as a wealthy speculator in Mexico in order to see the conditions on the plantations at first hand. In fact, the book had such an impact that Diaz felt compelled to announce, in an interview in 1908 with the American journalist Robert Creelman, that he would not be standing again in the presidential elections of 1910. Soon after the interview was published he changed his mind.

13 See the exhaustive and unequalled J Womack Jr, *Zapata and the Mexican Revolution* (New York, 1971), pp42-43. Any analysis of Zapata must and does draw heavily on Womack's careful researches. So accurate was it that the Mexican government refused him entry after its publication!

14 On the economic history of Mexico in general, E S G Garcia, *Cantu El Socialismo en Mexico Siglo XIX*, is central. On the revolution, A Knight, *The Mexican Revolution* (Cambridge, 1986) is a very complete and thoughtful analysis from a fairly formal historian's point of view.

15 By then Mexico boasted five individual properties of over 11.5 million acres. On the other hand there were just under 49,000 small farmers compared with one and a quarter million in 1960. Some 77 percent of

only to foreign capital and to that tiny percentage of the population who constituted the landowning class. Primary industries had grown (mining, oil extraction, steel) but were overwhelmingly in foreign hands. The oil industry, for example, was a battleground between Pearson, later Lord Cowdray of Mexican Aguila, and Josephus Daniels of Standard Oil. The mines were largely American owned, as a strike at Cananea in 1906 had underlined. When miners struck against the high prices charged at the company store, 500 agents of the American Pinkerton Agency[16] were brought in to deal with them.

Social tensions mounted during the first decade of the 20th century. In the areas where the main commercial crops (sugar, coffee, tobacco) were grown expansion brought dispossession of the peasant communities. In the industrial areas the growth of a working class brought with it the first trade union organisation and the first major industrial struggles—in the textile plants of Rio Blanco (1907) and later among the railwaymen (1908). At another level, small and medium Mexican capitalists were growing increasingly restive at the absolute control exercised by foreign capital over the economy. And the repressive and undemocratic nature of the Diaz regime was also generating a significant political discontent within the middle classes.[17] This then was the context of the centenary of independence from Spain—a society of profound inequality where the appearance of modernity covered a yawning gap between that sector linked to the world market, and an impoverished and undeveloping area of subsistence agriculture and small artisan manufacture. Even sections of the landowning classes of the north, for their own very particular reasons, were growing irritated with Diaz's exclusive devotion to European capital and were pressing for a change.

All these forces gathered, and the pressure grew as the anniversary approached. Francisco Madero, oddball son of a wealthy landowning family, published a pamphlet calling for political democracy and free elections. But his was only one expression of a much more widespread social discontent. The Flores Magon brothers, working within the Mexican Liberal Party, propounded the ideas of anarchosyndicalism in their newspaper *Regeneración* and were influential in the early trade union organisations.[18] In the agricultural areas of the central region the peasant resistance and the rebellion of the plantation workers were beginning to cohere around the leadership of Emiliano Zapata. The one point of agreement for every sector was the need to bring about the end of the dictatorship of Porfirio Diaz—beyond that there was no consensus.

17 That discontent is discussed and described in the excellent J D Cookcroft, *Intellectual Precursors of the Mexican Revolution* (Austin, 1968).

18 Some of the writings of the Flores Magons in *Regeneración* have been collected under the title *Land and Liberty: Anarchist Influences in the Mexican Revolution* (London, 1977).

25

19 The general analysis that follows owes a great deal to A Gilly, *The Mexican Revolution* (London, 1983), the indispensable guide for socialists approaching the topic.

In fact the fall of Diaz was not the end but the beginning of the Mexican Revolution.[19] Francisco Madero announced his opposition to Diaz in November 1910. The dictator's resignation, under foreign and local pressure, followed soon after, and Madero came to Mexico to present himself in the presidential elections of 1911. But his political programme was limited entirely to political reform. After the departure of Diaz, Madero moved closer to those landowners who had grown tired of Diaz's arbitrary rule but treasured the state he had created for their protection. The fall of Diaz, however, had taken the lid off a boiling pot—and it was impossible to replace that lid now. In the southern central region Zapata's peasant armies massed under the slogan 'land and liberty', while in the north Pancho Villa led an army of rural workers and peasants which, though it was profoundly unclear about its political objectives, was resolute in its refusal to allow the land barons to retain power. In the cities a student movement protesting at the repression of ideas echoed the widespread rioting of the urban poor that occurred in the capital city in 1910-11. And the working class, in the struggles that preceded the fall of Diaz, had announced their arrival on the stage of history. No simple cosmetic reforms, nor even an extension of the suffrage, could contain such contradictions.

For Madero, the revolution meant only the overthrow of Diaz and the opening up of the political system, no more. For Zapata, and to a lesser extent for Villa, the revolution involved deeper and more far-reaching changes. When Madero demanded that Zapata lay down his arms, Zapata refused, arguing that the objectives of the revolution were still far from realised. Now the revolution entered its first real phase of struggle. For Madero, despite the fact that he is now hailed as the father of the revolution, turned against the social base of the revolutionary movement and formed an alliance with the old bourgeoisie to defeat Zapata and Villa:

With the sudden release of the Porfirista straitjacket in 1911, Mexico threatened to run amok. This is not what Madero had planned or intended; the wrong revolution was happening, led by the wrong people, in the wrong places.[20]

In May 1911 he signed the Ciudad Juarez treaty, consolidating the agreement with the bourgeoisie for a negotiated peace guaranteeing the limits of the revolution. With Madero now in the presidency, the federal armies moved against the peasant armies of the south and the disaffected rural workers of the north fighting under Villa's command. Zapata's response was his Plan de Ayala, which demanded the expropriation of the great estates and the redistribution of the land to the peasant communities or *ejidos:*

> *It was to be the political expression of the nationwide peasant revolution, embodying Zapata's historical intransigence in the face of the bourgeois state and its three successive governments: Madero, Huerta and Carranza.*[21]

As Gilly quite rightly stresses, Zapata was a revolutionary, but he was not a Bolshevik or a Marxist. Though his ranks included, for greater or lesser periods of time, a number of anarchist intellectuals, the declarations of his movement are those of a mass peasant movement. To the extent that Zapata advocated and practiced the democratic organisation of the masses of the countryside and fought the bourgeois state intransigently, he was a revolutionary. At every stage he rejected compromise, substitution or gradualism, and took clear positions of principle defended by mass insurrectionary action. In the years that followed the struggle at the heart of the revolution was between the bourgeois state defended by Madero, and the demand for 'land and liberty' and communal ownership of the land which struck at the very heart of the plan for Mexico's modernisation which Madero and those around him had in mind.

Ironically it was the government battle against Zapata which gave the old generals, and some new ones, the roots and the organisation with which to turn on

Madero in February 1913 when the counter-revolution under General Huerta tried to re-establish the control of the old oligarchy. Madero was quickly executed, and Huerta assumed the presidency. Deprived of Madero, who had sustained the alliance with the landed aristocracy, the Mexican bourgeoisie found itself weak and powerless. Huerta threatened to reimpose the old regime of Diaz, with its coterie of favourites tied to European capital. Yet the only weapon that could challenge, let alone defeat, the armies of Huerta were the peasant armies of north and south under the command of Villa[22] and Zapata respectively.

The overthrow of Huerta in July 1914 was a victory won by the great peasant armies sweeping into the capital from north and south. The bourgeoisie had no army, no state apparatus, no political party of its own. Its mass social base lay in the divided and impotent petty bourgeoisie and an equally divided middle class, the majority of whom had tacitly or explicitly thrown in their lot with Huerta or simply withdrawn in desperation from the struggle.[23] Carranza, a wealthy landowner from the northern state of Coahuila and a sometime state governor under Diaz, emerged as the inheritor of Madero's mantle. He set out to try and cobble together a new political alliance between the middle classes, the few

22 On Villa there is far more myth than history. Most writings about him seem to go back to books by M L Guzman, *El Aguila y la Serpiente* (1926), and *Memorias de Pancho Villa* (1930).

23 M Azuela's famous novel *Los de abajo (The Underdogs)* (1916) reflects this view.

24 Published in *Tierra y Libertad*, the catalogue of an exhibition of photographs from the Casasola archive published by Oxford Museum of Modern Art in 1985.

30

uncompromised remnants of the landowning class, and sections of the army. Yet when Huerta fell, Carranza was powerless to prevent the triumphant entry of the peasant armies into Mexico City, or the assumption of the presidency by an intellectual collaborator of Zapata, Eulalio Gutierrez, who wore the wide hats and leather leggings of the southern peasantry.

One of the most glorious manifestations of this extraordinary moment is a marvellous photograph, or series of photographs, which show Villa in his braid and blue uniform sitting laughing in the presidential throne, his leg over one arm of the chair. Beside him sits Zapata, stiff and unsmiling, staring with deep suspicion at the photographer. In the same series a group of peasants sit awkwardly at the lunch counter of a fashionable Mexico City restaurant while the startled working-class girls in waitress uniforms look on. Those two photographs speak volumes.[24] For they show two leaders capable of overthrowing the old oligarchy yet uncertain what to do next. For the tasks set by the revolution were incapable of completion, except by these two mass leaders who have neither considered nor prepared for the assumption of power. Villa is delighted with the trappings of the presidency, Zapata feels ill at ease in this redoubt of the bourgeoisie. Neither has given any thought to the base they need in the cities. In a sense they have brought their base with them, but it does not live here among the working class. Their political perspectives offer nothing to those workers. They have seized power, but cannot use it.

In this moment of equilibrium, of a balance between actual power and state power, Carranza and his cohorts must have understood that the historical initiative now lay with them.[25] Between January and August 1915 a ruthless military struggle took place between Carranza and his generals on the one hand, and Zapata and Villa on the other. For in January Zapata and Villa left the capital to return to their rural bases. This left a political vacuum in the capital while the struggle for power was fought in the countryside. While Zapata and Villa were never overwhelmed militarily, they were driven back into their fortresses, leaving Carranza to occupy the capital, and state power, in August.

Needless to say, the United States recognised Carranza immediately. But neither that nor the skill of Carranza's generals would have been enough to ensure their permanence:

The revolution had reached the highest point attainable under the existing leadership; and...the revolution would now start to decline, however great the heroic yet defensive mass struggles still ahead. All was written in the

25 As early as 12 December 1914, from his relatively powerless position in Veracruz, Carranza published his first governmental decree.

31

26 A Gilly, op cit, p172.

events of December 1914, although naturally no one was able to read the writing.[26]

These peasant generals had power, but they did not know how to use it or who to call upon for its defence. The working class, as well as the urban poor and the petty bourgeoisie, watched as the days passed with the capital under occupation. There was little disorder or danger, but neither did these classes experience much real change in their lives. Because Zapata and Villa had no programme of government they did not enact change, not even the land reform law so central to their struggle, and certainly no laws to protect workers or attack property. For the next nine or ten months, and indeed longer, Alvaro Obregon, Carranza's main general and real political strategist, set about filling the political vacuum. Whatever Carranza's class instincts, his class had lost power. Obregon represented the rising bourgeois and petty bourgeois forces, but unlike Zapata and Villa he did have a programme for power and pursued it relentlessly. Its first stage was to win the petty bourgeoisie and the leadership of the working class to the struggle for a new state and against the peasant armies. At this stage the issue was posed in terms of the need to re-establish central government control over an atomised and chaotic nation. In fact, it was clear to Obregon that the consolidation of a new

27 See A Gilly, op cit, chapter 8.

class in power and the founding of a new state would only be possible once the existence of an independent power represented by the mass revolutionary movements of Zapata and Villa had been completely destroyed and state power reimposed.

When Carranza entered Mexico City in April 1917 as the undisputed president of a new Mexico, it was testimony to the success of Obregon's project. In the intervening period Zapata and Villa remained under siege in their shrinking redoubts. There is clear evidence of the rapid political development that Zapata himself was undergoing in the Morelos fortress. But the moment had, in a sense, passed, and there was too much political confusion within his camp to produce a clear direction now. Yet Womack and Gilly[27] both show how radical experiments in new forms of social living were conducted behind the fortress walls, speaking volumes for the revolutionary potential of Zapata's movement. Yet all of this was taking place without the knowledge of the working class. Though there was political debate within Zapata's camp, it never extended to developing the political links between his Morelos redoubt and the workers of the cities. That was the key, and if Zapata and his political counsellors failed to understand that, Obregon certainly did.

It is one of the most tragic and paradoxical aspects of the Mexican revolution that the working class of Mexico City was persuaded by its leaders (among them Dr Atl, Rivera's pictorial mentor) to form so called 'Red battalions' to fight against Zapata. In 1915 and 1916 Mexican workers fought under petty bourgeois leadership in the ruthless struggle to destroy the peasant armies. And it was a battle without quarter.

How can such a thing be explained? The key fact is that these 'workers' battalions' were formed in the aftermath of a series of defeats. When the peasant armies of Zapata had no use for power, and made no attempt to address themselves to the concrete problems of the working class of the capital and other cities, when they clearly showed that they had no understanding of trade unions nor plans for their development, and when they offered no response to their desperate material needs, it became very simple to represent these peasant revolutionaries as the *enemies of the working class*. And when a wave of workers' strikes in the major cities in late 1915 met defeat after defeat, the promises of Obregon that the new state, the 'revolutionary' state, would offer reforms and guarantees in a new constitution seemed the best that could be achieved. That was certainly what the newly formed trade union bureaucracy was repeatedly saying. There seemed no alternative now. Later, in the constitution of 1917, the right to strike and to trade union recognition were enshrined in the famous Article 123. But the foundations of that much-vaunted victory were built of the remnants of the revolutionary vision of Zapata.

In a formal sense the Mexican Revolution ended in 1917. Zapata continued his struggle for another two years before he was betrayed and murdered at the Chinameca hacienda. Villa disbanded his 'Golden Army' and retired—he was machined-gunned to death by an unknown assassin in 1923.

The 'end', however, referred not to a cessation of hostilities, but to the effective military victory of Carranza and Obregon. In the course of the military campaigns they had also made significant political advances. The vacuum was now filled. But by what? The 1917 constitution expressed the political victory of a new class. It established the executive, the presidency, at the heart of the political system. For the new society and the new ruling class would have to be built *from* the state. The old rulers had gone. In some cases their property had been confiscated and passed to new ownership, mostly the generals of the new army. But in any event they no longer possessed political power. The new rulers were largely military men of varied social and class origin. What they controlled was a new and still unstable alliance of social forces.[28] If the old landowning class no longer had political power, the new bourgeoisie was still small and weak, still devoid of an independent economic base and still facing the task of economic transformation. The other element in the alliance was the working class, or rather the nascent bureaucracy of the trade unions, tied to the state and reinforced by it, occupying the role of mediator and negotiator between labour and capital. Crucially, they were an agency of the state—acting on its behalf and providing the guarantee, the absolute guarantee of its support for the project of national independence and capitalist development for which the new state stood:

The constitution was an instrument and an expression of an incipient bourgeoisie allied to the organised workers in the struggle against imperialism and latifundism. The constitution was an instrument for the development of capitalism, and the development of the country within the framework of capitalism.[29]

And it could not have been otherwise. For the last independent actions of the working class, the long and bitter strikes of the winter of 1915-16, had been brutally repressed in both Mexico City and Veracruz. The state gained the collusion of the trade union bureaucracy, which was anxious to break the political power of the syndicalist leadership of the strike movement. The political alternative—an alliance between the urban and rural proletariat and the peasant revolution—had been destroyed in that crucial December of 1914.

Between 1917 and 1920, with the last opposition dealt with, the institutional foundations of the new state were laid by the military reformists. More importantly, the social base of the new state was formed and reformed. With Carranza in power, Obregon, more than anyone else the victor in the savage war against Zapata, moved into prosperous retirement. Actually, he was merely standing back, watching Carranza's attempts to forge a compromise with the old ruling classes, secure in his political control over another political alliance which would soon establish itself in the post-revolutionary state. As Carranza's attempts failed, Obregon was gathering his forces and preparing his assault on power. It came in April 1920, when Obregon was able to present himself as the champion and leader of a new popular coalition against the fragments of the old ruling class grouped around Carranza.

Obregon drew, with a wonderful irony, on those who had inherited the mantle of Zapata, and who now gave him support against Carranza. He was assured of

30 In 1988 APRA occupied the government of Peru and despite its left-wing rhetoric on foreign affairs, relentlessly pursued its enemies within. D Hodges and R Gandy, *Mexico 1910-82: Reform or Revolution*, is just such an account of the Mexican Revolution. As they say in the opening page, 'The Mexican revolution is a substitute for socialist revolution in the Americas.'

38

the support and active organisational backing of a trade union leadership he had helped to create, and which was forged in the battle against Zapata. His respect for private property calmed the fears of the small and middle capitalists. And he spoke for the new army command, born in the revolution, its authority established in the fight against the revolution of the peasants. These forces were the basis of the new state, populist in its politics, nationalist in its rhetoric, yet pragmatic in its relations with an external capitalist market with which Obregon re-established formal relations in 1923.

What then was the nature of the Mexican Revolution? It created a state based on a coalition of a number of classes in which none was strong enough to impose itself over the others. The state sought to establish its right to control and direct the national economy, but to achieve growth through renegotiating the terms of its relationship with imperialism rather than challenging that relationship. In the Latin America of the 1920s the Mexican Revolution became a kind of alternative model of 'revolution' to the example of Russia, formalised into a politics for development expressed through APRA in Peru and similar organisations elsewhere.[30] It became a political model for the achievement of national emancipation, yet also a formula for state-led growth in collaboration with imperialism. It was 'a counter-revolutionary solution to the problems of Mexico's underdevelopment',[31] and one which placed an insuperable obstacle in the way of further social change. While the state could take the place of an active and dynamic bourgeoisie, and create a new ruling class, it could do so only by the ruthless suppression, veiled with populist rhetoric, of popular needs and demands in the pursuit of economic growth.

Yet all of this could not be further from the vision of history that populates Mexico's walls!

31 See, on the formation and character of the Mexican state, A Cordova, *La Formacion del Poder Politico en Mexico* (Mexico, 1972), and A Cordova, *La Ideologia de la Revolucion Mexicana* (Mexico 1972).

Man at the Crossroads, Palace of
the Arts, Mexico City 1934: 4.85 x
11.45m.

DIEGO RIVERA: THE MAN WHO PAINTED WALLS

How to paint a wall

The echoes of the artistic revolutions that had occurred in Western Europe and in the ferment of Soviet Russia were only heard in Mexico when the noise of revolutionary warfare had died down. Under the presidency of Obregon the artists returned, drawn back by the promise of state patronage for a great art project—the decoration of the walls of the new society.

When Diego Rivera returned by way of Italy in 1921, he might not have seemed the most suitable candidate for the job. His main companions in the project, Siqueiros, Orozco and Guerrero, all had some direct experience of the Mexican Revolution. Rivera, on the other hand, had spent the entire decade in France and Spain, and had a reputation as a skilful but minor Cubist painter. He had paid a prolonged visit to the frescoes of northern Italy, financed by the Mexican government via his good friend Alberto Pani, the ambassador in Paris. But he had produced little of note.

Indeed, there was very little in his work so far to indicate his Mexican origins at all. Born in 1886 into an active professional family, he had shown (like Picasso) considerable skill as a draughtsman from a very early age.

Rivera was admitted to the main art school of Mexico, the San Carlos Academy, at the age of 12. What he found there was a rigid academic regime slavishly imitating the classical painting of Europe. In this, as in every other respect, the Mexican bourgeoisie acted as a surrogate for Europe. Tied to Europe economically and politically, the Mexican ruling class celebrated that relationship in its cultural expression. Those who could not make the pilgrimage to Paris recreated, in Mexico, the (often imagined) environment of Paris—the elegant art deco shops of the capital, the arcades, the theatres and the parks. The only painter of repute in Mexico at that time, Jose Maria Velasco, painted tranquil landscapes in the classical vein, which bore no relation to the Mexican landscape on which they were sometimes reputedly modelled.

The mounting social tensions of the Mexican society of the turn of the century had their parallels in the cultural field. The stifling conservatism of the cultural establishment produced other kinds of rebellion—in the field of philosophy, in music, and above all in the field of art. A new principal at San Carlos, Antonio Fabres, brought with him a commitment to documentary style, but it proved so rooted in surface detail that the prevailing mood swung the other way, towards Impressionist experiment. Yet it was the arrival of Gerardo Murillo, who adopted the Aztec name of Dr Atl, that caused the greatest impact. He painted dynamic, emotive Mexican landscapes in bright primary colours. His landscapes and figures were radical, shocking, anti-academic, unrestrained and vigorously nationalist. On the other hand, the nation that he painted was ahistorical and mystical, a spiritual rather than a social statement.

Until 1915 Rivera was clearly influenced by the styles that surrounded him. His work flits from style to style, experimenting with Cubist optics here and paying tribute to El Greco there. He was reproducing, imitating and experimenting with *styles* and perceptions. His brief Cubist phase stems in the first place from his obvious admiration for its complexity and depth. Nonetheless, Cubism was more than mere style. It challenged the bourgeois reverence for the eternal truths, static subjects and forms of art. It drew craft and construction into the aesthetic temple, confused and melded styles, and called the materials of everyday life (newspapers, paint pots, wood and wallpaper) into the precious artist's palette. The Cubists were responsive to and celebrated change, the rich potentials that each new advance in science, technology or knowledge opened up. And they delighted in the discomfort of the bourgeoisie. Yet their critique did not lead to any alternative: 'They were not clear among themselves of the meaning of the future in which they believed'.[32]

Whatever Rivera claimed in retrospect, his radicalism throughout this period was restricted to his artistic practice. He took no part whatever in any of the political movements, in Mexico or Europe, which occurred during the same period. Indeed, his works contained no reference at all to his Mexican background until 1915, when he painted a highly stylised and symbolic canvas called *Zapatista Landscape*. But it is of profound significance that at this, the most bitter phase of the struggle of Carranza against the Zapatistas, Rivera should have presented a completely romantic and idealised portrait of Zapata. The Indian serape, the gun, the hat and the Atl-like symbolic barren landscape bore no relation to any associated reality. Neither Zapata nor his guerrilla fighters were Indians. The land they fought for was lush and rich. The suggestive piece of paper nailed to a wall at the bottom corner of the canvas suggests a political manifesto, but it has no words on it. If, as several critics assert, it was a sign of Rivera's longing for home, then it was 'home' recreated in nostalgia, and one very far from the ravaged rural battlefields that were its contemporary reality. The same symbols appear again in contemporary portraits of Mexican friends, yet each is a Cubist portrait

32 J Berger, *Success and Failure of Picasso* (London, 1965), p63. See too his epoch-making essay, 'The Moment of Cubism', first published in *New Left Review* and reprinted in J Berger, *Selected Essays and Articles* (London, 1971), pp133-163.

33 A good account of the time is
J C Orozco, *An Autobiography*
(Austin, 1972).

of multiple personality set outside locations in time or
space. Thus these Mexican symbols become labels, merely formal references.

Rivera returned to a project already under way.
He found Orozco and Siquieros already employed,
together with a number of others, by a ministry of education bent on a great art renaissance. The idea of a
series of murals had in fact been suggested in 1910 by a
group of dissatisfied students at the San Carlos Academy
(including Orozco) under the influence of the ubiqui-
tous Dr Atl.[33] But the plan was interrupted by the out-
break of revolution.

It was resumed by the education minister in the
government of Obregon (1920-24), the contradictory
Jose Vasconcelos. This extra ordinary self-publicist
wrote a series of autobiographies in which he described
himself as the 'Mexican Ulysses' (modesty is not a qual-
ity required of Greek heroes). Obregon provided funds
for an ambitious education programme to lay the basis
for obligatory statutory education and to recast the history and culture of Mexico in a nationalist mould.
Vasconcelos's ministry reprinted the classics in cheap
editions and commissioned new histories, geographies
and archaeologies to furnish the edifice of Mexican
nationalism. He claimed, in fact, to be 'the first imitator

of the good aspects of the Soviet regime',[34] and explicitly modelled himself on Lunacharsky. Presumably what he was pointing to was the ambitious Soviet intention to democratise the best of bourgeois culture, to make the classics widely available, to raise the general level of literacy correspondingly, and to harness the persuasive powers of the artists. But to what end?

The rhetoric referred to the forging of a national culture and the rediscovery of Mexican identity. The scheme could be described in a different way. The deep divisions and class hostilities exposed in the course of the Mexican Revolution had not been eliminated—only the capacity of workers to mount an independent political challenge to the new state had been undermined. But the contradictions and conflicts remained, and the social base of the new state was far from secure. Though Obregon had come to power with a promise of reform, a message of national independence and a rhetoric of 'popular alliance', that alliance had still to be formed. For the material basis of such an alliance—a generalised improvement in the lives of the mass of the working class, redistribution of land and the creation of a class of small farmers, together with modernisation and development on a scale capable of responding to the demands of the middle class—was a distant dream, not the reality of

34 See J Vasconcelos, *A Mexican Ulysses* (Bloomington, 1963).

post-revolutionary Mexico. For those whom Obregon had won to his camp in the wake of the revolutionary defeat, this 'revolution' offered only scarcity, hardship in reconstruction, and a new reliance on the very foreign capital whose control over the Mexican economy had provided the revolution with its overachieving anti-imperialist impulse.

Yet consolidation was a matter of urgency. The centralisation of power under the new ruling group was a first step in the foundation of a modern capitalist state, set within the framework of a continuing uneven relationship with imperialism. But such a state could not rest solely on the exercise of military strength. It required an ability to marshal and control a whole range of social forces, and to forge a unity or consensus between conflicting interests that could achieve their collaboration in the formation of the new state. The cement to hold together this alliance was the implantation of a shared ideology, a common set of values and beliefs enshrined in the state whose generalised acceptance of what Gramsci called a 'secular religion' would guarantee ideological hegemony to the new state.

This was the task set for the education ministry of Vasconcelos, and this was the purpose he communicated in his turn to those whom he charged to create the symbolic language, the icons and symbols, of this new religion. Had this been all they did, of course, the Mexican Muralist movement would have no place in the history of revolutionary culture, which it undoubtedly does. And the fact that Vasconcelos denounced the whole programme within two years of its inception suggests that it had, at least at times, a healthy critical and sceptical attitude towards the whole project. Yet the need for the creation of an identifiable language for the new state, a kind of symbolic justification for its existence, and an imagery of its cross class roots, proved greater than the head of state's revulsion at the language and ideas employed.

The first murals were commissioned for the Preparatoria (a pre-university school) in the centre of Mexico City. They caused enormous and persistent controversy. Yet they were very different from one another. The work of Jose Clemente Orozco, for example, owed most to a tradition of popular art, particularly caricature, whose source was the marvellous engraving and etching of the prerevolutionary journalist Jose Guadalupe Posada. It was Orozco who addressed the reactionary role of religion in his *Christ Chopping Down his Own Cross*. And it was Orozco who in a general sense was most brutally critical of the human costs of revolution for the working class. His radical individualism was compounded by his anarchist sympathies, and his work always displayed a sympathy for the poorest, the most wretched, the most abused, as well as a scathing wit at the expense of the rich and the powerful. In the end his quarrel was with power itself, and his scepticism was radical and deep. His most powerful painting is also his most tragic vision. In *La Trichera*, three anonymous peasant guerrillas lie slumped across one another, their faces turned away from the observer, their particular history lost in a gloomy and undefined background. That they fought is clear in the foreground, where the ammunition belts stand out against their skin, but what they fought for is long forgotten.

Orozco's often scabrous *Autobiography* shows him to be no friend of the bourgeoisie, no believer in reformers in power. His general sympathy for the poor and the exploited, and the sweeping humanism expressed in the Guadalajara murals like *Man's Victory Over Cancer* or the heroic *Man In Flames*, however, were always tempered by a profound and unyielding pessimism, which often led him to see clearly but never showed how such insights could change the world.

The second of the leaders of the movement, David Alfaro Siqueiros, contributed *The Burial of the*

Worker to the collective effort, signalling the assertively proletarian tone that marked much of his earlier work. His paintings are as extravagant as the artist was. In any event, in this period Siqueiros remained the theorist and organiser of the group. Later he led an attempt on Trotsky's life, and was until the end an unreconstructed Stalinist. As a muralist, his work is best summarised in his paintings on the walls of the interior of Mexico City's Museum of History. There the dominant protagonists are masses, sweeping crowds whose first rows are recognisable cartoons of each of the social forces involved in the process of change. The bourgeoisie, with their elegant clothes and twisted smiles, represent a kind of polished and stylised version of Posada's figures, but without the bite that Posada's drawings had because they responded to more immediate provocations. The sweeping masses of peasants are their antagonists, yet they carry no slogans or manifestos. They have an enormous moral force, yet they lack the metal of real struggle.

For both Orozco and Siqueiros, the mural has an allegorical power, a force of suggestion and symbol. And when Rivera first began to work with them, his first work was also symbolic of great truths and cosmic forces. They were painted in Mexico, but with no reference to time and place other than occasional anecdotal connections

35 For the murals see D Rochfort, *The Murals of Diego Rivera* (London, 1987), which reproduces most of the murals and provides a useful (if slightly historically confused) commentary.

36 His main work was called *The Decline of the West*. For its influence on Latin America see W Rex Crawford, *A Century of Latin American Thought* (Austin, 1968).

37 These and other seminal documents are reproduced in D Siqueiros, *Art and Revolution* (London, 1975).

52

with Rivera's 'crowded' personal life (from which most of his models came). His mural *Creation* summons those massive, sensual and mythic figures who also populate most of his Chapingo murals. They symbolise a series of abstract philosophical categories derived from the curious system of ideas put forward by Vasconcelos, Rivera's patron.[35]

In a sense the *Creation* mural, for all its powerful forms and creative integration with the architecture of the Bolivar Amphitheatre where it was painted, remained a grand abstraction, a kind of deferential gesture to the patron's belief in education and culture as the guarantee of human liberation. Vasconcelos was a cultural nationalist of a sort, but the source of his beliefs was bizarre. He was an admirer of Oswald Spengler, the German philosopher whose cyclical theories of history provided a reassurance that Europe was dying and the southern world set to take its place at the head of the historic table.[36]

But even as it was being painted another facet of Rivera's art was emerging. While Orozco was deeply sceptical of the political function of artists, Siqueiros had no such reservations. And it was he, not Rivera, who set out the political terms of reference for the movement in two documents.[37] The first, published in Barcelona in 1921, was his declaration of artistic principles, an attempt to integrate into one school of painting every aspect of artistic radicalism. It extended a vigorous welcome to Cézanne, to Cubism, to Impressionism. It expressed that admiration for modernity and the machine age which Cubists and Futurists had voiced in their very different ways. In the practice of art the emphasis would be on craft, with the artist as artisan. For its materials this new art would draw on motifs of ancient Mexican and African art, and take art beyond the boundaries of the frame and the easel.

It was these rather confused if exuberant precepts that were given more organised expression in the 1922 manifesto of the newly formed Union of Technical Workers, Painters and Sculptors, to which all the Muralists belonged. Their newspaper, *El Machete*, with its large and emphatic woodcuts and poster format, echoed the wall newspapers of ROSTA in Russia. The manifesto showed clearly why the government was feeling increasingly ill at ease with its new employees, for it combined the radical populist nationalism they might have expected with elements of a more radical perspective. In the manifesto the mural was not only to burst on to the streets—the artists were also to become proletarians, as an act of solidarity with the workers.

In its principles, the manifesto promised a new

38 Ibid, p24.
39 Ibid, p25.

practice of art (collective and workmanlike), a new scale of art (monumental, the size of public buldings), a new subject matter (the renovation of Mexican society), a new form (the mural), a rootedness in the national tradition ('the art of the Mexican people is the most wholesome spiritual expression in the world'[38]), and a new artist, repudiating easel painting 'and every kind of art favoured by ultra-intellectual circles, because it is aristocratic'. They praised public art as authentic social property and proclaimed a joint determination to 'produce ideological works of art for the people'.[39] The signatories included Orozco, Siqueiros and Rivera.

The question, of course, was what ideology these works would embody. But the answer was embedded in the text itself. The subject of this ideology was 'the people', its expression 'the nation', with a continuity of cultural expression through time. This was a subtle but important shift from the revolutionary declaration that Siqueiros had made only a year earlier. Here was continuity in place of rupture—the artists were now integrated into the nation. Beyond that, painting (and the artist) became public property, that is, the property of the state.

It was at this stage that a noticeable cooling of relations began between the government and the painters. After its fifth issue *El Machete* became the official newspaper of the newly formed Mexican Communist Party, which Siqueiros, Rivera and Xavier Guerrero joined in 1922. Not only did they join it, but they became three sevenths of its executive committee. Clearly then there was no conflict between the overt nationalism of the Muralists, albeit couched in radical populist terms, and membership of the Communist Party.

What did all this mean for Rivera's practice? While still painting the *Creation* mural, Rivera was sent to southern Mexico by his ministerial patron. He returned with a new set of colours in his palette and a new vocabulary of images. Rivera had discovered the Indian. The final panels of *Creation* embraced lush images of tropical vegetation and the Indian figures that were to become so much his mark. For his move into Mexican art was through the Indian, the idealised representation of suffering, oppression and nationhood. At times, of course, Rivera would paint workers in struggle and the urban masses, but the central idiom of his work remains that symbolic language of nation encapsulated in tropical landscapes and archetypal primitive figures.

To reinforce the point, although there was much talk in the manifesto of identity with the popular tradition, Rivera did not noticeably employ the elements of an authentic popular tradition in his work. The idealised

Indian corresponded to an abstract idea of nation coined above all by the rising middle class redefining itself in its opposition to imperialism and its allies among the old bourgeoisie. The popular tradition, on the other hand—and it was an extremely lively one in Mexico—embraced popular music, caricature, popular theatre and above all the radical journalism of people like Filomeno Mata and the savagely critical engravings of Posada. And of the three leading muralists, it was undoubtedly Orozco who most directly emerged out of that tradition.

The year 1923 marked the beginning of the most creative phase in Rivera's life. Given the commission to paint Vasconcelos's ministry of education building, he set out to produce a rich and comprehensive panorama of Mexico's past and present. It was to take five years and produce 116 major mural works of the highest level of technical skill. They were a powerful, sympathetic narrative of a people's history. In that same period Rivera's relations with the other Muralists grew more tense, as Orozco and Siqueiros were gradually refused further government contracts, and Rivera became the sole organiser of the great mural project. Orozco's growing disillusionment has already been mentioned. Siqueiros was moving increasingly towards an explicitly propagandistic style which Vasconcelos found intolerable. So when the murals of Orozco and Siqueiros at the Preparatoria were attacked with hammers and chisels early in 1924, Vasconcelos's successor at the ministry was ready to bow to such shows of public pressure.

Yet Rivera seemed immune from these criticisms. Clearly both his interpretation of the aims and practices of the Muralist movement were closest to what was expected of it. The ministry of education provides almost a summary of those aims and images. In the Court of Labour, Rivera painted 18 frescoes, depictions of agricultural and industrial life in Mexico. The first series derives directly from his trip to southern Mexico, and presents in stylised form the women and the society of Tehuantepec in southern Mexico. On the east wall the two most overtly political panels address the experience of the miners. In *The Entry* bowed miners trudge down into the belly of the yawning mine which consumes them. In *The Exit* a miner is searched by the foremen at the surface, his arms raised in an attitude of crucifixion. In a later panel, the curiously named *Liberation of the Peon*, an armed soldier holds his companions' horses while they lie down and cover the naked body of a dead peon, its attitude that of the Christ figure taken down from the cross that Rivera must have seen in so many Italian murals. The peon's hands are tied—he has probably been shot, and his face is obscured. The religious echoes in all three paintings are inescapable. As a history of injustice they are telling and powerful. But they are also compellingly fatalistic, passive and without response. The workers have the status of victims, the Indians are picturesque but impassive and idealised. And if the ninth panel, *The Embrace*, is intended as a pointer to the future, then the unmistakable halo around the peasant's head and his priestlike garb and stance suggest a reconciliation in sorrow, a shared despair. There is nothing here of joint action.

In the *Court of Fiestas* the tone is more vital, more celebratory. Yet it is also anthropological, an exploration of curious exotic residues of that same ancestral culture. The celebration of All Souls Day, the Day of the Dead, when Mexico is full of strange dancing skeletons made of cardboard or sugar, makes a colourful symbol of popular rejoicing. Yet it should be contrasted, too, with the work of Posada, for whom the Day of the Dead symbolised the deepest contradictions in Mexican society. His *calaveras* (dancing skeletons) are not picturesque bits of folklore but savage satirical commentators on hypocrisy and exploitation. Against that, Rivera's nativist portraits are inescapably bland and timeless. The market, the ancient dance of the deer, the festival of maize, all are chosen to symbolise more than anything else the stability of the

Aztec world. These are the main features of the popular Mexico that Rivera offers.

The revolution is present too. In the mural called *May Day* a colourful cross section of Mexican society, workers and peasants, gather under a banner that says, 'True civilisation shall be the harmony between man and the earth, and between man and man'. This points to the centrality of the Indian as ancestor or as peasant in the work of Rivera. These crowds of faces standing watching the May Day celebration or the ceremonies of land distribution are, in conjunction with the others in the same court, still lifes in human form, representations of life in a timeless place, an Eden lost and regained. Their symbolism, though the themes are secular, is religious, their form is statuesque, their function is iconographic. This is the creation of a language of symbolic forms, recurring in different times and places so that they become, in some way, the substitution of the eternal nation for a religious eternity. They are moving because the peasant and the Indian have not figured in earlier Mexican art. They are disappointing because these representatives of the masses are still without life, without dynamic, without intervention in their own world. It is worthwhile, for example, to compare with them the extraordinary murals at the Chapingo Agricultural

College, painted concurrently with those of the education ministry.

In the chapel at the college Rivera creates a secular place of worship (if such a thing is possible). The religious icons are replaced with huge sensuous Mother Earths, and curious representations of Zapata and his lieutenants lying dead beneath a soil fertilised by their sacrifice. Again and again the theme is of sacrifice, of an earth fertilised by martyrs' blood, of a cycle of death and rebirth. And in the mural *The Distribution of the Land at Chapingo* it is striking how passively the crowd stands, hats in hand, receiving from the representative of the state their right to the land. Only *he* seems active, knowledgeable and to be pointing ahead to the future.

Who, then, is the protagonist of these murals, or indeed of the third series which illustrate the history of the Mexican Revolution through the ballads, or *corridos*, which were its songs? There is a mass—passive, expectant, and striking attitudes not very different from those who sit in the timeless landscapes of the Indian past or who strike the static poses of the Renaissance icons. On the other hand, there are the individual heroes—linked always to sacrifice and death, whose example has a powerful moral force. Like the Christian martyrs they act *for* the waiting people and seek to rebuild the shattered nation crystallised in the symbolic figure of the Indian, represented in an attitude of patient expectation.

There is a later, and famous, series in the Court of Fiestas (1926-28), which come much closer to an agitational art, (pages 3 and 5). The panel showing *The Wall Street Banquet* is contrasted with the simple fare of *Our Bread*, where bread is broken at the head of the table by a smiling revolutionary. Revenge is sweet when the bourgeoisie must sweep the floor in *He Who Eats Must Work*. And in *United Front* there is a stylised representation of the unity in struggle of worker, peasant and soldier.

Powerful, amusing and moving though these murals often are, they remain static allegories, caricatures in the widest sense of the men and women who occupy the walls. We are offered a panorama of Mexican life distilled into precisely those of its features which are timeless and universal. Within the nation are preserved and reproduced the eternal verities that Rivera found in the Renaissance frescoes of Giotto. Is it too cruel a comment to note that Rivera became in 1925 the editor of the vigorously folkloric magazine *Mexican Folkways*? Was that what was meant by the notion of a monumental art—a representation of eternal and founding truths? In Rivera's case that is what it came to mean, but that was not the implication it had in the 1922 manifesto.

40 J Berger, *Art and Revolution* (London, 1969), p55.

Was this a revolutionary art, as has so often been claimed? Clearly it was an idealisation of the image of nation and people purveyed in the political rhetoric of the new state. But if a revolutionary art renders 'the complexities and contradictions' in society, 'not ironing out the ambiguities but containing and defining the totality in which they exist',[40] then Rivera is the least revolutionary of them all. In his paintings the conflicts of the past are resolved in the present. The harmony of the past is recaptured in the state's embrace of peasant and worker.

Outside the ministry, as he was painting, a counter-revolutionary religious war was being fought against the new state. Yet while the state closed the churches and pursued the priests, President Calles's wife continued to hold mass in her private chapel. And the continuing anti-imperialist rhetoric of government statements did not prevent Calles or his government from working in close accord with the US government and creating the conditions for the return of foreign capital to Mexico in the process. Yet Rivera dealt neither with these immediate contradictions nor with the long term conflict between the aspirations of the peasants whom he so lovingly portrayed and the demands of a resurgent export agriculture. It is a culminating irony that one of his finest expressions of the historical experience of conquest and occupation, the Cuernavaca Palace murals, should have been commissioned (ie paid for) by US ambassador Dwight Morrow as a 'gesture of personal gratitude to the Mexican nation'.

As an example of monumental art there can be few more impressive than Rivera's major mural work, the three enormous panels in the National Palace depicting the history of Mexico. Their composition is of mind-boggling complexity—the whole history of Mexico from conquest to the eve of the Cardenas government of 1934 is represented. There is here a movement, a dynamic, a sense of forces at work, which is absent in his earlier work. In the retrospective exhibition of his work, for example, a sketchbook of his visit to Moscow on May Day 1928 shows great columns of workers and soldiers sweeping along the street. These are no longer representative individuals nor bland icons. Here at least (ironically, given the significance of the year 1928 in the chronicle of Stalin's rise to power) is some sense of the forces that shape history.

Yet still Rivera has not reached through to any sense of the collective. Outstanding individuals represent the struggles for Mexican independence, from the Spanish conquest to 1910, in the great central panel on the main stairway. On the right, the Aztec world is shown as both idyllic harmony, a group centred on the religious cultural figure of the plumed serpent and quetzalcoatl, and as a society of primitive violence, sacrifice and a naked exercise of power. In the huge central panel a circular core represents the eagle and the serpent, symbol of a Mexican nationhood rooted in the Aztec past. Rising from the centre to the central arches, the heroes of the struggle from independence to revolution are crowded together, looking outwards. To left and right, from bottom to centre, the Jesuits' enforced baptisms, the horrors of the conquest, the inquisition, the enslavement of the Indians in mines and fields, are shown through stereotypical representatives of these confrontations. And there is, at the bottom, an undoubted feeling of struggle, of a power imposed and savagely enforced. Yet at the top the placid pantheon of heroes and leaders imposes itself again, reaping the harvest of these struggles while the anonymous peasant armies look on.

As a history of the Mexican revolution, as a representation of the circumstances of the birth of the new state, it is a hagiography, a celebration of its origins. A monument, yes, but a bourgeois monument. History, yes, but a bourgeois history of great individual heroes and a *self*-motivating progress. Time progresses by itself, and there are victims and beneficiaries.

The third panel was painted three years later, in 1933, under the title *Class War*. At the apex of the mural Karl Marx stands pointing to a future of industrial expansion and growth. Beneath him the bourgeoisie and their servants conspire, corrupt and accumulate within a symbolic factory. Outside the workers and peasants reach up towards the vision that Marx proposes. This, at least, uses the language of class and identifies in ways closest of all to the great caricaturist Posada the twisted faces of the bourgeoisie and the proletarian character of their antagonists. Yet even here the conflict is avoided as the workers rise above and beyond the bourgeois edifice to reach the portals of a bright future promised by Marx. At the height of the mural is one of the tenderest moments in the mural, as peasant and worker clasp hands on the threshold of the future.

Diego Rivera enjoys a worldwide reputation as a revolutionary both because of his political history and because of his art. Yet he was someone who learned his politics through his art and not vice versa, and whose work ultimately contributed most to the creation of a myth of Mexican nationhood of which only the present repressive Mexican state is the beneficiary. It is true that he and his wife Frida Kahlo opened their arms and their

Rivera (top left), with André Breton (fourth from left), Frida Kahlo (right) and Leon Trotsky (bottom left), Mexico City, 1938.

REVOLUTIONARY PORTRAITS

house to Trotsky when no one would take him in, and it is true that he was denounced by the Stalinist establishment as a Trotskyist. He certainly admired Trotsky, as he admired all great figures, and he occasionally put his name to articles exposing the crimes of Stalinism. Yet Rivera's natural home was in the Mexican Communist Party, in which, on and off, he spent the best part of his politically active life. For it was there that a visionary commitment to the future social harmony to match or reawaken the harmony of the primitive Indian community could be reconciled with nationalism and an alliance of classes against imperialism. Rivera, if his work is a guide, could never be at ease with Trotsky's internationalism nor, above all, with his resolute commitment to the self-emancipation of the working class.

Rivera continued to paint and develop his mural style. He was a master of his craft, a fine teacher and a skilled draughtsman. His journeys to America in the early 1930s produced a fine set of murals in Detroit depicting the growth of industry with an unparalleled sense of the power of the machine. Yet time and again those ancient universal symbols reappear, now disguised as machines, and the cycle of life, death, sacrifice and heroism is evoked again and again. Of course no one who offended Rockefeller so deeply with a tiny picture of

Lenin in the corner of a mural commissioned by the old thief can be all bad. Yet it is ironically a charming but shallow mural for which Rivera is best known. *His Sunday Afternoon at the Alameda Park* brings back simultaneously the pantheon of heroes of Mexico's national struggle. At the centre stands Rivera himself, playfully depicted as a boy holding the hand of an overdressed skeleton. Around him are the assembled inhabitants of his book of history, looking outwards from a flat wall. The mural has no depth, no perspective or sense of change, only an endless accumulation of experience captured in the unchanging face of the nation.

In the final analysis it is against every principle of socialist culture to proscribe appropriate forms and subject matter for a 'socialist art'. To do so leads to the idealised little Stalins which populate the hundreds of worthless social realist portraits of Russia. The mural is no less or more revolutionary a form than a photograph or a newspaper. But there is something invigorating and positive to see the public spaces occupied in our society by exhortations to buy, impossible images and dreams of unattainable consumption replaced by a celebration of ordinary life. The crowded, exuberant panoramas of Rivera are rich in poignancy and horror. They yield up all sorts of images to feed our rage or raise our conviction—the grimacing Cortes, the hurt worker, the determined revolutionary hero. Above all, at their heart is a collective presence, and that is their most forceful answer to the individual consuming a bottle of rum on a lonely beach who occupies our hoardings. And the vicious caricatures of Rockefeller and Morgan are weapons in our arsenal.

To the extent that these great monumental works enthuse and amuse us, they are grist to the revolutionary mill. Yet the contradiction is that their very power has come to be used in the service of a falsification, for the paintings invariably lead us from conflict to a harmony achieved, or at least promised, as inevitable because such is the movement of technology or knowledge of history itself. Thus in the end his crowds, his masses, are always spectators, waiting for history to happen. The relationship between the spectator and the work of art is one that reinforces and echoes the deeper message about the relationship between workers and their history. For revolutionaries, it is of their making. It must be not just understood or learned, but enacted. Rivera's paintings in the end use the symbols of universal truth to turn the transient domination of a bourgeois nationalist state into yet another eternal truth. His paintings lack contradiction or paradox. Yet that must be the central experience of every worker facing the capitalist class—and nowhere more so than in Mexico, where the symbolism of revolution and the mask of Zapata are systematically employed by a ruling class that persecutes and murders those who are still fighting to complete the Mexican Revolution.

The Making of a Fresco, Showing the Building of a City, San Francisco Art Institute, 1931: 5.68 x 9.91m.

For other publications from Redwords go to:
www.redwords.org.uk